WHAT YOU NEED TO KNOW
BEFORE YOU START A BUSINESS

Printed and Bound in the United States of America
Published and Distributed by:
Professional Publishing House

Cover Design: Kevin Allen
Formatting:**Professional Publishing House**
First Printing,
10 9 8 7 6 5 4 3 2 1

ISBN# 978-0-9826704-0-8

Library of Congress Cataloging-in-Publication Data

What You Need To Know Before You Start A Business, Dr. Rosie L. Milligan
and Clara Hunter King, Esq.

Professional Publishing House
1425 W. Manchester Blvd., Suite C
Los Angeles, CA 90047
www.professionalpublishinghouse.com
drrosie@aol.com
(323) 750-3592

Clara King
www.claraking.com
(770) 981-3243

WHAT YOU NEED TO KNOW BEFORE YOU START A BUSINESS

ROSIE L. MILLIGAN, Ph.D.

CLARA HUNTER KING, ESQ.

PROFESSIONAL PUBLISHING HOUSE
LOS ANGLES, CALIFORNIA

NOTE

This book is a general guide to help you get started in your business. The principles are applicable to starting a business in any state. Any specific laws and code sections quoted in this book are based on Georgia and California laws.

It's always a good idea to "sit down and count the cost" before embarking on any new endeavor. Starting a business doesn't have to be difficult, but you must do your homework before you begin. It will make your passage smoother as you glide through the maze of government red tape that all new entrepreneurs are confronted with.

We recommend that you check with your family attorney, tax advisor, and financial planner so that you are armed with all the information you need to get off to a good start. It always costs more money to back track and make corrections and adjustments in a new business than getting professional assistance up front. Remember to work smart—not hard.

In Loving Memory

Of

Our Father

SIMON OWEN HUNTER

He was a real entrepreneur.

He was a farmer who owned his own farm;

A tailor who made his own suits;

and a speaker who wrote his own speeches.

TABLE OF CONTENTS

I. INTRODUCTION

here has never been a better time to own your own business. Even if you have a job that you love, it's a good idea to investigate business opportunities and seek other sources of income. Most of us have heard stories of individuals who showed up at their place of employment, only to find the doors padlocked and the employees wondering what happened to their paycheck. Because job security is a thing of the past, you are wise to turn your thoughts in the direction of a new venture that can be profitable and rewarding. The fact that you purchased this book is a step in the direction of making your dream of owning your own business come true.

This book will provide you with information on where to get the permits, licenses, and identifications numbers you need to get your business started. It provides step-by-step checklists for the various types of businesses you should consider, along with the advantages and disadvantages of them.

There are many laws and rules that apply to all businesses, regardless of the size. Learning all you can about the requirements to get started in business before you sign a lease or plunk down a deposit on a building will go a long way in helping you to succeed. You can save money, time, and avoid frustration by finding out the specific requirements for opening the type of business you want at the location you have chosen.

Government regulations seem to increase each year. The forms are longer, and the fees are higher. The more information you have before you take the plunge, the more likely you are to have a profitable and satisfying business venture.

Once you have chosen the type of business you want, read everything you can about it. Study those who succeeded in the business as well as those who failed. Knowing what "not to do" can be a very valuable lesson.

If you investigate, plan, study others, meet all the requirements of the regulating government agencies, jump in with both feet and work hard, you are bound to succeed.

A Well-Structured Business Plan Is a Must

IF YOU ARE not able to prepare a business plan for yourself, seek help. The Small Business Administration has seminars on preparing a business plan. You should participate in the preparation of your own business plan so that you can understand what you are about to embark upon. After all, you know more about your vision and dreams than anyone else.

A business plan is to a business owner what a blueprint is to a builder. It helps you to answer these important questions: Where you are going? What will you need to get there? Who will you need to help you get there? How much will it cost to get there? Will you have access to the funds to get there? Who will your customers be once you get there? How much will it cost to draw customers to your business? With all these pieces in place, you can clearly determine if this is the business venture you want to embark upon now, or if you need to delay it for a while.

COUNT THE COST BEFORE YOU DECIDE TO BECOME THE BOSS! Bottom line: do not quit your job, invest your retirement funds, or mortgage your home before preparing a well thought out business plan. You need a road map that you understand. You must be willing to make personal and financial sacrifices to get where you want to go.

II. PRE-BUSINESS FOOD FOR THOUGHT

he most important decision you can make in starting a business is to be sure you are living your own dream. Far too many people start a business based on suggestions by well-meaning friends and relatives who think they would be good in a certain trade or business.

In a seminar entitled "Erase No ... Step Over Can't ... And Move Forward With Life," the participants were asked to participate in an exercise called "Are You on Your Own Agenda or Someone Else's Agenda?" Soft music was playing while each participant meditated on the issue. Then the question was asked—for each participant to ponder, not answer—"If there were no risk, what would you be doing right now as it relates to your occupation?"

When the exercise was over, each participant was asked to open his/her eyes. The emotional impact was overwhelming. Many participants were asked to share with the group their experiences. Ninety-five percent of the participants discovered that they were on someone else's agenda.

Why not try the exercise yourself and make a note of what you are feeling. Then you will be able to answer the most important question. *Is the business you have chosen really YOUR choice?*

Business Scenarios

NUMBER 1:

PAMELA STARTED BAKING as a teenager. She was stroked over and over by her parents and friends. The praise she received was so rewarding, Pamela would bake anytime she was asked.

Her mother encouraged her to start baking wedding cakes. Pamela tackled that with great success. All of Pamela's relatives and friends decided that she should open a bakery. Baking had only been a hobby for her. However, Pamela was talked into opening a bakery. The once-loved hobby turned into a nightmare. You see, operating a bakery was not just baking cakes and pies. There was inventory to control, pricing products for profit, negotiating with vendors, and supervising employees.

Pamela could not continue charging her relatives and friends the previous prices charged when she was working out of her home. Yet, Pamela's relatives and friends could not see paying more for their cakes and pies now. Sound like a problem?

NUMBER 2:

JOHN STARTED WORKING on cars at an early age. He became the family mechanic. Family and friends relied on him to keep their automobiles running. They would buy the parts—John provided the labor. John's father thought it was best for John to open up a mechanic stop—so he did. John found that there was more to a mechanic shop than repairing automobiles. There was pricing for profit, inventory control, etc. Last, but not least, relatives and friends wanted to pay the same low price for labor as before John opened the shop, before he had all those extra expenses.

NUMBER 3:

ROSA OPENED A clothing and accessories boutique in her home. Relatives, friends, and church members patronized her faithfully. They all thought it was time for Rosa to move her business away from her home. Rosa took their advice (remember, none of those with opinions had ever owned a business in their home, nor away from home). Former customers found it hard to make it to Rosa's store during her business hours. They would sometimes call and ask if she could bring panty hose home for them. The customers wanted to continue purchasing Rosa's clothes on credit, depleting her inventory, leaving her without the cash needed to reinvest in inventory. Relatives, friends, and church members could not see paying more for Rosa's merchandise just because she moved from her home to a building.

NUMBER 4:

LINDA ALWAYS WANTED to be a teacher—she loved teaching. After teaching for 10 years, she was burned out. She decided to get into the insurance business. Linda's husband and relatives concurred that it was outright ridiculous for her to just up and throw away her career and all those years of college to sell insurance, which requires no degree. They also asked about her retirement and insurance benefits. Linda quit her job, started her insurance business, created her own retirement plan, is paying for her own life and health insurance, and is creating the wealth she had always dreamed about.

NUMBER 5:

DR. BOONE HAILS from a family of physicians. He has a great practice as a neurosurgeon. He keeps abreast of medical trends. He is cognitive of the fact that the majority of patients in this country will soon be affiliates with some health maintenance organization. He also realizes that if he became too ill to work, even for a short period of time, his lifestyle would change drastically.

Dr. Boone decides to take a look at a multilevel marketing company. He understands the principals of

O.P.M. (other peoples' money), O.P.E. (other peoples' efforts), and O.P.T. (other peoples' time). When he shared his excitement with his family and coworkers, they said, "You are a doctor; you can't lower yourself to become a peddler, peddling products. After all those years of hard work and the time you spent in medical school—Doc, stick with your practice!" The outcome of Dr. Boone's dilemma will be revealed in Volume 2.

Many people often get hobbies mixed up with vocational occupations. Author Marsha Sinetar wrote a book entitled, *Do What You Love, The Money Will Follow.* If you do what you love and the money doesn't follow, it's probably a hobby and not yet a business.

Licenses and Permits

WHETHER YOU PLAN to open a small business or large business, conventional or home-based, start from scratch or take over an existing business, certain standard actions must be taken before a product or service can be sold to the public.

Cities and counties require licenses and permits to be sure you comply with local ordinances. If you are within the city limits, you will need a business license or permit from both the city and the county. If you are in an unincorporated area of the county, you will not need a city license.

Both the city and county will require you to pay a fee to operate your business. You will usually be given the choice of paying a flat fee or an amount based on the percentage of your gross receipts each year. Some cities will require you to pay a license fee in addition to a percentage of gross receipts.

When applying for a license, you will need to go in person to the Business License division and complete the application. Your application will then be processed through the zoning or planning department. The zoning or planning department will check to be sure that your location and building meet all the zoning requirements for your intended use before the license is issued.

Home-Based Business

IF YOU WISH to operate a home-based business, you'll need a city license if you live within the city limits, and a county license if outside the city limits. Your home address is your business address. Most cities and counties will not allow you to use a post-office box as a business address. You can always use your home address as your mailing address.

In some counties, an additional charge will be added to your property-tax bill when you operate a home-based business. This charge is an annual fee to cover the cost of additional garbage pickup at your home as a result of the business.

Businesses That Are Conducive To Home-Based Operations

FOLLOWING IS A list of activities that are conducive to home-based businesses. They do not require clients to come to your place of business. A home-based business may be service or product-oriented. Often, service businesses such as multilevel marketing and direct sales products are sold at the clients' home or place of business. For these types of services and products, it is not cost-effective to pay for office space when you can operate a successful business from your home.

Accounting Services	Advertising Consultant	Answering Service
Appliance Repair	Architect	Audio Taping Service
Billing Invoice Service	Bookkeeper	Bridal Consultant
Carpenter	Child Care	Clothing Alteration
Computer-Related Services	Consulting	Courier/Messenger
CPA	Cosmetologist	Data Processor
Designer	Desktop Publishing	Editor
Educational Consultant	Engineering Consultant	Entertainer
Event Planning	Fashion Consultant	Financial Planner
Floral Arrangement	Gardner	Graphic Designer
Housekeeping Service	House Painter	Image Consultant
Import	Insurance Agent	Interior Designer
Janitorial Service	Laundry Service	Locksmith
Mail Order	Musician	Photography
Piano Tuner	Plumber	Teacher
Proofreader	Publishing	Real Estate Broker/Agent
Repair Service	Sales Representative	Secretarial Services
Sign Painter	Speaker's Bureau	Tax Preparation
Telemarketing	Tutorial Service	Typing Service
Upholstery Cleaner	Videotaping Service	Window Washing Service
Writer	Yard Service	Medication Transcription
Legal Transcription	Credit Repair	Dating Service
Grant-Propoal Writer	Health Food/Menu Analyst	Home Inventory Service
Resume Preparation	Data Researcaer	Book Formatter
Ghost Writer		

Zoning and Planning

REMEMBER, ZONING ORDINANCES can be a big issue when a new facility is to be constructed or when an existing building is to be used for a different purpose than the previous use.

If your business location is not zoned for the type of business you plan to open, you will not be able to get a license for the business. If you have already signed a lease, you may have to change your application to the same type of business as the previous owner. But beware: Even if you decide to operate the same type of business as the prior owner, don't assume that you can just open up shop and start doing business. Check to be sure you can get a license for the location. Some businesses are "grandfathered in" (i.e., they were operating their business before a more stringent law was passed). It may be that the new owners must meet different requirements in order to operate the same type of business at that location.

Before you spend large sums of money on signs for your business, you should check the city or county ordinances to see if the type and size of sign you have in mind is permissible at that location.

Help Is Available

MOST FIRST-TIME ENTREPRENEURS feel lost when dealing with the enormous amount of red tape involved in starting a business. They are not aware that advice and support are available from both the government and private sector. You can get valuable information and assistance from the Chamber of Commerce, Community Development Departments, Civic and Trade organizations, and the United States Small Business Administration (SBA). The entrepreneur should join the local Chamber of Commerce, attend business mixer network meetings, and check the SBA Web site for topics ranging from buying an existing business to writing a business plan. At www.sba.gov, you will find a wide range of topics providing information you need when starting a new business.

Find a Mentor

ONE OF THE best ways to get your business off to a good start is to talk with people who have gone before you. You don't have to reinvent the wheel. Learn from their experiences. Regardless of what you have heard about busy, successful business owners, you should approach them with an open mind and a positive attitude. Most successful businesspeople are eager to help others. State right up front that you are planning to start a business and would appreciate any assistance or information they can give you. Don't become discouraged if you encounter a businessperson who is not willing to share. You will find that more are willing to help than not. When you find someone willing to share their experiences with you, ask them if they would be willing to answer some questions that you feel would help you in getting your business started. If they are not, just get as much information from them as you can and move on.

The following page is a list of questions you should ask if they agree to speak with you. Modify the questions to fit your needs.

Questions to Ask Your Mentor

1. How long have you been in this business?

2. Is this your first business venture?

3. Why did you choose this business?

4. How much money did you have to put into this business for start-up?

5. Was your start-up money enough to operate effectively?

6. Where did you get your start-up money?

7. How long was it before you could take money from the business for personal use?

8. What other source of income or support did you have while getting your business off the ground?

9. Did you start your business full time or part time?

10. How many hours a day do you spend working your business?

11. Is this about the right amount of hours you had expected to spend?

12. How does this business impact your family life?

13. How does this business impact your social life?

14. Was your business designed to include family participation?

15. Were your family members trained to work in your business?

16. How did you go about choosing your business location?

17. Did the location turn out to be the right one for you?

18. Who did you expect to be your customers?

19. Who were your customers and what mile radius did they come from?

20. How did you go about getting customers?

21. What worked best?

22. Was your business in the community where you lived?

23. Were you known in the community where your business is located?

24. How did you make yourself known to the community?

25. What type of media did you use for advertising?

26. What worked best for you?

27. Do you feel that you had adequate skills to handle your business?

28. Was your college or vocational education geared to your present business or previous businesses?

29. Did you contact a business consultant?

30. Do you feel that a consultant did or could have enhanced your business success?

III. REASONS TO
OWN A BUSINESS

Keep More Money in Your Pocket

 business of your own is still the best way to help you keep more of your money in your pocket.

As an owner of your own business, you can benefit by hiring your children. Hiring them is a win-win situation. You are giving them money anyway—this way, they can work for it. Working gives the child a sense of pride and keeps more of the would-be tax dollars in your pocket.

You can pay your children a salary and still claim them as dependents on your tax return as long as you paid more than half the cost of their support during the year. Your children, in turn, must file their own tax return, claiming zero dependents. But their standard deduction may be limited by the fact that they can be claimed as dependents on your return. The exact amount of their standard deduction must be determined by means of an

IRS worksheet. It's always a good idea to figure it both ways to determine which is more advantageous.

If you have a room in your home that's used regularly and exclusively for business activities, you may deduct a percentage of mortgage interest and property taxes, utilities, telephone, home insurance, and other expenses in maintaining your home on your business tax return. You may also depreciate a portion of your home as a business use of home expense as it relates to the percentage of square footage used for the business.

There are two methods of deduction regarding the expenses for the business use of the home. These methods center on the square footage of the home or the number of rooms in the home. Here's how it works: If your house is 1,500 square feet, and you use 300 feet for business, your business usage is 25 percent. On the other hand, if you own a five-room home (and all rooms are approximately the same size) and use one for your business, your business usage is 20 percent.

You may deduct personal computers and other business machines and equipment used in the business as depreciable items, even though you do not take a deduction for business use of your home.

If you use your automobile in your business, you can take a tax deduction for automobile expenses. For example, if you operate your automobile 70 percent for personal use and 30 percent for business use, you can take a deduction of 30 percent of your actual operating costs, or take a depreciation deduction based on the percentage of business use.

Business Verses Hobby

A HOBBY IS something you do because you enjoy it. While you might, and should, enjoy running your business, it's something you do because you want to make money. The IRS estimates that incorrect deductions of hobby expenses account for a portion of the overstated adjustments, deductions, exemptions, and credit that add up to $30 billion per year in unpaid taxes. The IRS presumes that an activity is carried on for profit if it makes a profit during at least three of the last five tax years, including the current year. If you continue to operate a business that does not earn a profit year after year, it may be classified as a hobby and you may lose your business deductions, retroactively.

So, if you have a hobby and it turns into a money-making venture, apply for a business license and report it as a business on your tax return. Consider the lady who once made rolls in all sizes and shapes for her family. The neighbors started to purchase them and told their friends and family about them. Pretty soon, she had more orders than she could handle. During the holiday season, she had to hire two other individuals to help her. She was able to deduct the expenses of all of her supplies and utensils because she made a profit each year. Her hobby turned into a profitable business. If you have a hobby and it doesn't make enough to pay for the expenses associated with it, you can't take a deduction for those expenses, and you don't need to report the money you make from it on your return. It's just a hobby.

Now that you know some of the hurdles that you must jump through in order to get your business started, you can decide what type of business structure you want. Following is a list of the business structures to choose from. You should consider the advantages and disadvantages of each and choose the one that best serves your business purpose.

IV. CHOOSING A BUSINESS STRUCTURE

Sole Proprietor

s a sole proprietor, you are the only owner. You make all the decisions, own all the profits, and owe all the debts of the business. There is no one to disagree or throw a monkey wrench in your plans or hinder you in pursuing your dream. For tax purposes, you and your business are one and the same. The major change will be the addition of a Schedule C Form 1040 to your tax return to show the income and expenses of the business. If your business earns a profit, you will figure your self-employment tax on Schedule SE of Form 1040. You can report your business income under your Social Security number if you have no employees. However, if you hire employees, you will need to apply for an Employee Identification Number to report their income.

The primary disadvantage of owning a sole proprietorship is that creditors can come after your personal assets to satisfy the business debts. If they are awarded a judgment against you, they can attach your bank account, grab your debt-free automobile, or place a lien on your house. If you close the business while you still owe business debts, you are still personally liable for the debts. Also, you can be personally liable if someone is injured at your business location because you didn't use reasonable care to maintain a safe place for customers. You can purchase personal liability insurance to cover injuries to customers or damage to their property. The insurance will pay the cost of defending the lawsuit and any judgment, up to the limit of the policy. This is especially important if you have a business that lends itself to risk for your customers. For example, your business may have constant spills where customers can slip and fall. You should also consider insurance to cover your personal assets in case someone wins a judgment against you as a business owner.

Don't get in too far over your head. If the business is not working, get out before you sink too deeply in debt, work out a plan to pay any lingering debts, and move on with your life. Many successful entrepreneurs didn't succeed their first time around. If you are determined to own your own business and make realistic plans, you will succeed eventually. When you compare the risk of failure in business to losing your job in today's economy, owning your own business can't be too bad.

See Appendix A For A Start-Up Checklist For A Sole Proprietor

General Partnership

A GENERAL PARTNERSHIP consists of two or more owners who manage the day-to-day activities of the business and share in the profits and losses. While it's not required, it's always a good idea to have a written partnership agreement. The terms and conditions of oral agreements tend to be forgotten. Your partner won't remember the terms when disputes arise. If the partners don't sit down and write up the terms and conditions to govern the business, in a dispute, the outcome may be determined by state law. It's called the Uniform Partnership Act, or the Revised Uniform Partnership Act, and you may be unhappy with the outcome. For example, in some states, the partnership is automatically dissolved if one partner leaves, unless the remaining partners vote to keep the partnership going within 90 days. With a written agreement, you decide how the partnership is terminated.

As with the sole proprietor, creditors can come after your personal assets to satisfy the debts of the partnership. Judgments and liens are against the partners in proportion to their ownership in the business. If one partner signs a contract on behalf of the partnership, it binds all the partners as well as the partnership. That means the creditor can come after the business or each one of you individually. The same applies for injuries to customers or damage to their property while on the business property.

The partnership files its IRS informational tax return on Form 1065 to show the income of the partnership. Each partner will show his loss or profit on Schedule E of his individual tax return. If a partner has passive losses (such as income from real estate investments or royalties) from the partnership, he/she can only take a loss against that income from other passive investments. Other than the partnership agreement, the paperwork for a partnership is basically the same as for a sole proprietor.

A well written partnership agreement covers:

- Name of the Partnership
- Business Purpose
- Definitions
- Capital Contributions
- Duties of General Partners
- Allocations of Profit and Losses
- Distributions/Reimbursements
- Compensation
- Resolving Partnership Disputes
- Liability of Partners
- Termination and Dissolution
- Sale of Partnership Interests
- Powers and Obligations of General Partners

See Appendix A For A Start-Up Checklist For A Partnership

Limited Partnership

A LIMITED PARTNERSHIP includes the attributes of both a general partnership and a corporation. There must be at least one general partner and one or more limited partners. The general partners manage the business activity while the limited partners invest in the business but are not involved in the day-to-day operation of the business. The general partners are personally liable for the business debts. The limited partners, on the other hand, are not liable for business debts and their loss risk is limited to what they have invested in the business, so long as they do not take part in managing the business. Some states require limited partnerships to file registration information with the secretary of state about the general and limited partners.

As with the general partnership, the limited partnership files its return, Form 1065, but pays no tax. The profits and losses are reported on the individual tax returns of the partners.

See Appendix A For A Start-Up Checklist For A Limited Partnership

Corporation

A CORPORATION IS a separate legal entity from its owners. In other words, it's an artificial person. Corporations are formed by filing the required forms with the secretary of state and publishing a notice of intent to incorporate in the legal newspaper for the county where the corporate office will be located. A corporation is owned by its shareholders and managed by individuals elected by the shareholders. The corporate officers are usually a president, vice president, secretary, and treasurer.

A corporation can be established by any number of individuals or only one individual. The corporation files its own tax return, Form 1120, and pays tax on any profits. Profits can be distributed to shareholders as dividends. If the corporation declares dividends for the year, they are taxable to the shareholders even if they are not distributed. Dividends are not deductible as a business expense on Form 1120. So the corporation pays tax on the funds, and the shareholders pay tax on the same funds on their individual tax returns. This is a form of double taxation. Officers, shareholders, and employees of the corporation are not liable for the debts of the corporation and can only lose the amount of money they have invested in the business.

But beware; if you guarantee a note personally, as some banks require when making a loan to a corporation, you will be on the hook for the debt if the corporation can't pay the loan.

When forming a corporation, you should beware of a doctrine called "piercing the corporate veil." This refers to removing the "umbrella" that shields the shareholders and officers from any debts and judgments against the corporation. You can take steps to prevent someone from piercing the corporate veil by doing business in an equitable manner, not attempting to defraud creditors, following the guidelines of your state for operating a corporation, and keeping the business of the corporation separate from your personal business in every way.

See Appendix A For A Start-Up Checklist For A Corporation

S Corporation

AN S CORPORATION is established and operated much the same way as a regular corporation. The S corporation is a domestic corporation that is eligible to elect to be treated as an S corporation and makes the election by timely filing IRS Form 2553. Unlike the regular corporation, the S corporation does not pay tax on its income. Form 1120S is used to file the federal tax return, and the profits and losses are passed through to the shareholders and reported on their individual tax returns. The shareholders are not liable for the debts and claims against the S corporation.

Some limitations of the S corporation are that it can not have more than 100 shareholders, it can only have individuals as shareholders, and it can only have one class of stock. There are other requirements you must meet before electing to become an S corporation. Please check with your tax advisor before attempting to make the election.

See Appendix A For A Start-Up Checklist For An S Corporation

Limited Liability Company (LLC)

AN LLC IS a legal entity established by filing Articles of Organization with the secretary of state in the state where the business is located. The owners are called members and may run the business themselves, or hire someone else as manager. As with the partnership, the profits and losses of the LLC are passed through to the members and taxed on their returns. The LLC can opt to file its return as a corporation (Form 1120) or partnership (Form 1065). A single member LLC will usually report his income as a sole proprietor on Schedule C of Form 1040. As with the corporation, a single individual can form an LLC. If the LLC has more than one member, you will need an operating agreement. This document specifies how the business will be managed, profits and losses allocated, disputes settled, and methods of transferring membership interest.

See Appendix A For A Start-Up Checklist For A Limited Liability Company

Exempt Organization 501(c)(3)

WHILE AN EXEMPT organization is not in business to make a profit, it's listed here because it can pay its employees a salary and fulfill rewarding charitable purposes for the organizers, and those who make contributions can take a deduction on their tax returns. An exempt organization must be formed for religious, charitable, literary, scientific, or educational purposes. An exempt organization is first incorporated in the state in which it will operate and then applies for exempt status with the IRS. This is done by filing IRS Application 1023. An exempt organization is not required to file a tax return or pay taxes if its income is under $25,000. However, you may be required to file an annual electronic notice (e-postcard) Form 990.

See Appendix A For A Start-Up Checklist For An Exempt Organization

As with all corporations and limited liability companies, members, owners, and workers should keep their personal financial affairs completely separate from their business affairs.

NOTE: If an exempt organization is dissolved, any funds remaining must be given to another exempt organization.

Other Business Structures

There are other business structures to consider when starting a business, but they are usually for such professionals as doctors, lawyers, and accountants. They are: professional limited liability companies (PLLP), limited liability partnerships (LLP), and the professional corporation (PC). Just be aware that they exist. They will not be addressed in this book.

V. HIRING EMPLOYEES

Food For Thought

mploy a family member whenever possible. Even though you view your business as a small business, structure the operation the way you want it to be when it has reached its full potential. (Don't look at your business as it is today, but look at your business as it will be tomorrow.)

One of the most common mistakes made by small businesses employing relatives is that the relative is placed on the job without the proper skills and orientation. As a result, frustrations mount because the family member feels inadequate and you become irritated because it seems that the person cannot do anything right.

When employees make an error, show them how to correct it. Don't correct the mistake yourself while you angrily murmur under your breath, "I'll do it myself." Allow them to make the correction under supervision.

Treat your family members the same way you treat all other employees, including paying them on time.

Practices to Follow with Employees

1. Application and interview

2. Reference check

3. Complete W-4 Forms (Declaration of Exemptions & Dependents)

4. Independent Contract Agreement if non-employee status

5. Sign-in sheet or time card; have employee sign the time card, etc.

6. Have the employee sign a job description after it has been thoroughly reviewed

7. Hire all employees on probationary status (3 to 6 months)

8. Do monthly evaluations during the probationary period

9. Evaluation appraisals should be objectively oriented

10. Have the employee complete his/her own evaluation form just to see how he rates himself

11. When evaluating an employee who is not doing well, use the sandwich approach. Begin your comments with a positive statement, place the negative statement in the middle, and conclude with a positive statement. Try to catch the employee doing

something right and give him/her praise. He will usually become a better employee, and you will be a happier employer.

12. Develop an intense 2-week orientation program for employees with a checklist to be signed by the supervisor and employee.

Employee Orientation Checklist

1. I have read my job description and reviewed it with my supervisor and fully understand my job duties.

2. I have been orientated to all equipment I'll be working with and understand the equipment functions.

3. List the equipment including telephone system, alarm system, etc.

4. I was allowed to give a hands-on demonstration of all equipment I'll be using in my work.

5. I understand the chain of command when faced with a problem.

6. I agree to follow the standards of the company and keep the company's best interest in mind for the duration of my employment.

7. All company business shall be held in confidence when/where applicable.

_____   _____
Signature   Date

Who Are Employees?

IT IS IMPORTANT to understand the difference between an employee and an independent contractor. Never allow an employee to decide that he/she is an independent contractor. Request *Publication 15, Employer's Tax Guide*, which clearly defines an employee, at irs.gov, or call 1 (800) 829-3676.

Per IRS guidelines, anyone who performs services is an employee if you, as an employer, can control what will be done and how it will be done. This is so even when you give the employee freedom of action. What matters is that you have the legal right to control the method and result of the services.

Generally, an independent contractor is a person in business for themselves, and you pay that person to perform a service for you. This person has no ties to you and offers his service to the general public. After the job is finished, you may never see the independent contractor again, or you may call the contractor again in the future. An example would be a pest control service, lawn care service, a mobile computer repair service, or a typing service that picks up the work and brings it back to you.

Treating Employees as Non-Employees

IF YOU TREAT an employee as an independent contractor, and IRS determines that he is, in fact, an employee, you will be liable for both your share and the employee's share of Social Security and Medicare tax, as well as the federal income tax that you did not withhold because you treated him as an independent contractor.

If you are unable to determine whether the individual is an employee or an independent contractor after reading Publication 15, you and the individual can complete IRS Form SS-8, Determination of Worker Status for Purposes of Federal Employment Taxes and Income Tax Withholding, and send it to the IRS for a determination. While you are waiting for the determination, it's a good idea to go ahead and withhold the taxes. It will be easier to make the adjustment later if the individual is determined to be an independent contractor.

VI. KNOW YOUR TAX OBLIGATIONS

egardless of the structure you chose for your business, you need a working knowledge of federal and state tax laws. The tax returns needed to report income from your business are covered under the checklist for business structure types above. However, if you hire employees or contract with independent contractors, there are additional tax requirements you must fulfill. The withholding requirement forms for all business types are basically the same when you hire employees or engage independent contractors.

Federal Taxes to Be Withheld or Paid by the Employer

- **Federal Income Tax**—To be withheld from the employee's wages based on the information reported to you on the employee's Form W-4 for federal tax, Form G-4 for Georgia state tax, and DE 4 for California state tax.

- **Social Security Tax (FICA)**—The current rate is 15.3%. This consists of 7.65% (a combination of 1.45% Medicare and FICA of 6.2%) to be withheld from the employee's wages and the matching share of 7.65% to be paid by the employer. The maximum amount of FICA on which you withhold from the employee's annual wages varies from year to year. However, the 1.45% for Medicare does not have a limit and is paid by both the employee and the employer. The rates for Social Security are subject to change each year. Use IRS Form 941 or Form 941 EZ to figure and pay this tax.

- **Federal Unemployment Tax (FUTA)**—The Federal Unemployment tax is not withheld from the employee, but is paid solely by the employer. The rate is 6.2% of the first $7,000 earned by the employee each year. Figure and report this tax on Form 940 or Form 940 EZ.

- **Independent Contractors**—If you pay an independent contractor $600 or more during the tax year, you are required to issue him a Form 1099 MISC at the end of the tax year. You report this income to IRS just as you report the wages on Form W-2 for your employees.

- **Federal Tax Deposits**—You must deposit the taxes you withhold from the employee and your share in a financial institution, usually a bank, in a timely basis.

- **Note:** If you are responsible for depositing or paying the withheld taxes to IRS and fail to do so, you can be personally liable for the taxes. If the business fails and ends up in bankruptcy and all the other debts are discharged, you will still be on the hook for the withheld taxes.

- **Publication 509**—Tax Calendars will provide you with all the due dates for filing returns and depositing taxes. You can obtain them at irs.gov or call 1 (800) 829-3673.

VII. A HINT TO THE WISE

Checklist

- Plan your work and work your plan.

- Get to know your bankers well.

- Do not wait until you need money to seek a loan from the bank.

- Have employees bonded when handling cash, even a relative.

- Carefully choose your partner. It is not a casual relationship. Before signing the agreement, get to know your potential partner's spouse and children and their attitudes and behaviors. Which spouse is the decision maker?

- Find out about the credit rating of your partner-to-be.

- If a general partnership, make sure the partner has as much to lose as you do.

- Agree on how much time each partner will give to the business.

- Make sure your partner can pay his/her personal expenses without depending on income from the business for the first 12 months.

- Make sure your short-term and long-range goals are the same for the business as your partner-to-be's.

- Decide who will get paid from the business, when, and how much.

- Work out a responsibility description and put it in writing.

- Last but not least, if you don't know what you're doing, ask somebody who knows.

VIII. MARKETING FOR PROFIT

How to Outsell Your Competition

t would surely be nice if all businesses could afford public relations or advertising specialist personnel. The reality for most small businesses is that the owner finds him/ herself wearing all the hats. Unfortunately, for many of the hats he/she takes on, that individual has not had training or experience to handle such positions.

You must clearly define what it is that you have to sell. Is it a product, information, service, or an idea; or, is it a combination of the above? Remember, customers buy your products because of the service that goes with the product. Make "service first" your daily motto and number-one priority.

It is important to get inside information on your business competitors. Below is a list of ways to obtain information regarding your competition's products or services.

1. Go directly to the company yourself as a research student.

2. Send an employee or friend to the company.

3. Watch your competitor's advertisements in newspapers, etc.

4. Check with the Better Business Bureau for information.

5. Check Dun & Bradstreet for information.

Business Name

WHAT'S IN A name? This question has been asked for centuries. You should be cautious about tying your legal name (i.e., your own name) to your business. Your name may be impressive to you and to the person who gave you the name. Unfortunately, during the course of your business venture, you may have a lawsuit or charges brought against your business that may impact your business image. Remember, it is more convenient to change a business name than your own name.

A business name should really have a significant meaning. In other words, it should depict your service or product. After all, a business name is a very important marketing and advertising tool.

Business Cards

YOU MAY WANT to have more than one set of business cards. There are times when it becomes necessary to inform the person with whom you are negotiating that you are the proprietor, president, or CEO. There are also times when your status can be an asset; and there are times when it can become a liability. Remember, ego is not the substance that closes the deal. Also, you may be the only person impressed with your ego. When someone gives you a business card that reads, *"John Doe*, President or CEO" and they are really the sole proprietor with no employees, *that's* ego.

Fancy business cards are great. You must keep in mind that a business card is a great marketing and advertising tool. Make sure the color is easy on the eye and the print is readable. The name and slogan used should depict the product or service you provide.

If you are operating a home-based business, you may not want to use your home address. The use of an address does lend itself to more credibility; therefore, you might want to use a post office or mailbox service with an address or suite number instead of P.O. Box number.

A business card should have a phone number. If you are operating a home-based business, you may not want to use your personal telephone number. Voice mail is always appropriate.

Business Grand Opening

MANY SMALL BUSINESSES open a new business in the community with a fabulous "Grand Opening!" with food, games, fun, laughter, networking … truly a day of festivity. However, days and weeks following the grand opening, there may be little business activity. **WHY!**

The open house was not objectively oriented; therefore, the people left not knowing what the business owner wanted or expected from them.

You must tell people what you need them to do for you. You must always ask for business. Do not assume that everybody knows that you want and need their business.

Remember, an open house or grand opening is not just a meeting-and-eating gathering. Invite people who have influence in the community. Send invitations to celebrities asking them to attend. On your flyer or announcement, list the celebrities as invited guests.

Whatever your agenda may be for your grand opening, etc., make sure it is customer-driven.

Here are some ways to get customers, keep customers, and have customers get you more customers. Stroke their minds. Remember, "Customers will pay more for *service* than *products*."

⇨ Refer clients to your customers when applicable.

⇨ Remember clients' birthdays, anniversaries, etc.

⇨ Inquire about the things they love and enjoy (children, animals, etc.).

⇨ Send a "I Miss You" card if you haven't seen them for quite some time.

⇨ Send clients information that can benefit them and their families (coupons, clippings from papers, play or movie recommendations).

⇨ Take a photo with clients for your portfolio.

Ways to make the community feel like a part of your business:

⇨ Create a board.

⇨ Participate in Block Clubs.

⇨ Speak at PTA meetings.

⇨ Speak at local churches.

⇨ Support neighborhood Little League teams, etc.

⇨ Canvas the community and introduce yourself.

⇨ Hold a "Get Acquainted Celebration."

⇨ Recognize a community worker.

Here are ways to keep your image before the public:

⇨ Write press releases.

⇨ Place activities in newspapers under Calendar of Events.

⇨ Have your photo on press releases, flyers, brochures, etc.

Public Relations & Advertising

NEWSPAPERS, RADIO, AND television talk shows are always in need of helpful and useful information to pass on to their listeners and viewers. Develop a press release centered on an issue that is of interest to the public and mail it to newspapers, magazines, radio, and TV talk shows. Continue to mail press releases. Do not become discouraged, and remember that persistence pays. Your local television stations always need guests on their shows. Call all the local TV stations and cable stations because they need people like you. You will gain much credibility with your customers as a result of them seeing you on television or hearing you on radio or reading about you in the newspaper, etc. Always include a black-and-white picture with your press release.

Remember, marketing is to a business what oxygen is to the heart and brain—it keeps it alive and functioning.

According to Jay Conrad Levinson in his book, *Guerrilla Marketing*, the 10 truths you must never forget are:

1. The market is constantly changing.
2. People forget fast.
3. Your competition isn't quitting.
4. Marketing strengthens your identity.
5. Marketing is essential to survival and growth.
6. Marketing maintains morale.
7. Marketing give you an advantage over competitors who have ceased marketing.
8. Marketing allows your business to continue operating.
9. You have invested money that you stand to lose.

10. Marketing does not always bring instant gratification.

Remember, the key to success in marketing is not always how many new customers you get, but how many customers you keep. Customers are necessary for a viable business; therefore, you should concentrate on customers and "customer-getters." Customer-getters are customers who get you customers; i.e., they will refer others to you or bring them to you.

IX. WAYS TO INCREASE PROFIT

 ood For Thought:

1. Offer incentives for clients who give you referrals.

2. Send a thank-you card to your clients who made referrals.

3. Send a miss-you card to your clients you have not seen for a while.

4. Have some type of reception once a year and invite your clients and their guests.

5. Check competition fees for services and products.

6. When you cannot be competitive, give away specialty items with purchases.

Common Sense Do's & Don'ts

Do's

1. Set a price for your products and services that will yield a profit.
2. Have a suggestion box for clients.
3. Listen to employees' and clients' concerns.

Don'ts

1. Allow family and friends to just drop in to chat if you have a home-based business.
2. Allow people to just hang out at your business.
3. Allow time-snatchers to snatch your time.
4. Allow clients to call you at home when you have established office hours.
5. Take office work home.
6. Allow clients to just freely use your telephone & fax machine.

Tap into the Internet

The Internet is fast becoming an economical way to market your products and services. You can market your business on the Internet even if you are on a shoestring budget. There are individuals who will set up your

Web site for as little as $250. You can save even more by registering your domain name, choosing a hosting company, and setting up your own Web site. It's a fairly simple process, and you will be proud of yourself when you view your site.

Before setting up your own Web site, check out the Web sites of other businesses similar to yours, both large and small. Navigate through their sites to see how easy or difficult the journey can be. It will give you an idea of what to do and what not to do when setting up your own site.

Once your site is up and running, you must find a way to draw people to it. One way to do that is to register with as many search engines as possible. Google is the most popular search engine and perhaps the best place to start when looking for information on search engines and marketing on the Internet. Many newcomers have made millions on the Internet. Give it a try—you could be next!

X. USING YOUR HOME TO FINANCE YOUR BUSINESS

Look Before You Sign

 f you make a decision to mortgage your home in order to start a new business or take over an existing business, there are some key points you need to keep in mind.

When you are required to sign documents, you are usually giving up some rights in exchange for property, money, or privileges. The person presenting those documents to you should explain, in plain English, the purpose of each document. While most of us do not take the time to read all of the documents when purchasing a house, automobile, or business, we should be sure to look at the name/title of each document before signing. You should be sure you know what the document is and what rights you are giving up before you sign it.

Get It in Writing

REMEMBER, WHEN YOU enter into a written agreement, verbal promises made by the presenter are not binding and you have no legal recourse if they are broken. If you and the other party discover some additional terms or information that should be a part of the agreement/contract, put it in the writing. At the very least, the change or additional terms should be written on the document and initialed by both parties. If you are dealing with real property and the change is an important term, have those responsible redo the documents to incorporate the changes. It's better to wait a few days to complete the transaction than to lose thousands of dollars in the future. Don't forget, talk is cheap. It doesn't cost the other party anything to make you an oral promise, but it can cost you thousands if you take their word for it and they don't fulfill their word.

Critical Documents

FOLLOWING ARE SOME documents that should always get your attention because they are an indication that your real property (house) is involved. Take a good look at the figures and the name and address on these documents. Remember, if the other party doesn't have the time to allow you to review the documents, you should reschedule the closing to a more convenient time. It's your money or property at stake. Don't allow them to rush you. Besides, if they don't want to allow you time to review the documents, that's an indication that something is wrong.

1. **Mortgage/Trust Deed/Deed To Secure Debt:**Whenever you see a document titled Mortgage or Deed, it is very likely connected to your real property. This is the document that creates the lien on your property and says that you can lose your home through foreclosure if you do not make your loan payments. If you determined that this transaction involves your real property, be sure you review the following documents carefully.

2. **Promissory Note/Note:** This document shows the amount of debt you promised to pay, and attaches the mortgage to the deed.

3. **Truth In Lending (Disclosure):** This document shows the annual percentage rate, the amount you are borrowing, the total finance charges you will pay if paid according to the terms of the loan, and the monthly payment amount.

4. **Hud-Settlement Statement:** This document shows all the closing costs and how the proceeds of the loan will be distributed.

5. **Riders/Adjustment Riders**
   Variable Interest Rate
   Fixed/Adjustable Rate Loan Principal Dwelling Program Disclosure

Any document with the above heading or any combination of the above headings under paragraph 5 should be reviewed carefully. These documents describe the features of any variable rate program connected to the loan. Pay close attention to the sections that show *How Your Interest Rate Can Change and How Your*

Payment Can Change. Many people lose their homes each year because they did not understand or were not aware of the fact that their mortgage contained an adjustable or variable interest rate.

For example, Mrs. Smith was awarded her personal residence in a divorce case. The mortgage was $845 monthly at the time of the divorce. She refinanced the house to reduce the mortgage to a monthly payment that she could afford. At the closing, she understood that her new mortgage would be $615. What she did not understand about the adjustable rate was that it was tied to the LIBOR (London Interbank Offered Rate) index rate and could increase every 6 months. After 3 years and four increases, she could no longer afford the mortgage and suffered a foreclosure.

When refinancing real property to start a business, be sure you have a fixed interest rate. However, if you choose an adjustable interest rate program, be sure you clearly understand the terms and can afford any increase in mortgage payments.

If you are not sure your loan interest rate is fixed, ask the presenter to show you the document and the line on the document that states that your interest rate is fixed. If you don't feel comfortable with the closing documents, it's a good idea to have them reviewed by a real estate attorney. Remember, the person handling the closing does not represent you.

Check the Attorney's Complaint Record

IF YOU HAVE an uneasy feeling or are unhappy with how things are going with the attorney handling your closing when refinancing your home to start your business, check out the attorney's record with the bar association.

A. Bar Association

You can call the state bar association (phone number is on the Web site) to check out the discipline or complaint record for attorneys in your state, or check them out on the Internet. Go to www.calbar.org for California, www.gabar.org for Georgia, or go to Google and put in the name of the state and bar association you are seeking.

- Click attorney resources on left
- Click attorney search on left
- Click attorney/member search
- Type in attorney's name
- Click on attorney's name to view his/her record

B. Better Business Bureau

You can check to see if a complaint has been filed against an attorney, or any other person with whom you are doing business, through the Better Business Bureau.

C. Get Another Attorney

If you are unhappy with the services provided by the attorney handling the refinancing of your home in connection with starting your business, get another attorney. You are entitled to have your current attorney return all your important documents to you.

XI. BUYING AN
EXISTING BUSINESS

Check Out the Neighborhood

heck out the neighborhood where you are considering establishing your business, visit several times and at different times during the day, and talk with people who live in the neighborhood before making any decision.

Get Prior Year Tax Returns

GET A "TRANSCRIPT" of the last two tax returns of the business to verify the income. The current owner can provide this for you by completing Form 4506T (get a copy at irs.gov, or call 1 (800) 829-3676) and request that IRS mail it directly to you. This includes specific information, such as the adjusted gross income and taxable income. Remember, if the seller provides you with a copy of his return himself, if may be "fixed."

If your business is different from that of the prior owners, be sure to check with the business licensing department to be sure the location is zoned for your type business. Too many first-time entrepreneurs sign a lease and take over a business before they obtain a license. If this happens and you can't get a license for the business you had in mind, it may not be easy to break the lease.

Get a Copy of the Deed

WHEN BUYING OR selling real estate as a part of your new business venture, it's important to get a copy of the DEED that's attached to the property. A deed will always be involved when real estate is transferred from one person to another. Hire a business consultant, a tax accountant, and a real estate attorney when purchasing a building in conjunction with an ongoing business. After all, it costs money to start a business, but it will cost less to get professional help in the beginning rather than later.

Other Important Details and Documents

WHEN PURCHASING AN ongoing business, be sure to do the following and check these documents and files:

- Personnel records if you plan to keep existing employees
- Have an electrician check all electrical hookups and lines
- Have the water company check water pressure and lines

- Have an inspection of roof leakages and beams for water damage
- In California, have the structure checked for earthquake cracks
- In Georgia, check basements for flood damage
- Request copies of insurance premium rates for the business

Before purchasing any business that includes the building, get an appraisal. A business appraisal costs more than a regular home appraisal, but it's worth the extra funds to be sure you are getting what you pay for. If the business requires the use of a great deal of water, such as a carwash, check out the utility bills for the last several months. This information will be needed when you prepare your business plan.

You Can't Buy Customers

WHEN PURCHASING AN existing business, you should be aware of the fact that people are loyal to a person more often than they are to a business, especially when personal services are involved. Take the example of Wendell who purchased a carwash from John. He learned too late that the customers were loyal to John, rather than the carwash, and followed him to the new location he opened in a nearby area. Also consider the example of Sarah, who purchased a thriving beauty salon from Joann. Both Sarah and Joann felt sure all of the customers would remain with Sarah since Joann was retiring. After a few months, however, the customer base began to dwindle. Sarah didn't know what happened to the customers. She only knew they didn't come to her beauty salon and didn't return her phone calls.

In conclusion, we urge you to check ALL available information about the type of business you want to operate, the location of your choice, and talk with other businesspeople in the neighborhood. After you have investigated everything you know to investigate and asked everyone you know to ask, then pray, make your decision, and then jump in with both feet. We wish you a successful, profitable, and satisfying business venture.

APPENDIX A
BUSINESS STRUCTURES

START-UP CHECKLISTS FOR EACH BUSINESS STRUCTURE

Start-Up Checklist For Sole Proprietor:

1. **Business License**—from the city or county in which you will do business.

2. **Employer Identification Number (EIN)**—If you do not hire employees, you can use your Social Security to file your tax return. If you hire employees, you must apply for an EIN. Use IRS Form SS-4 to apply for an EIN. You can print the form at irs.gov, complete it, and call 1 (800) 829-4933 to get the EIN by phone, or mail the application to the address on the form.

3. **Fictitious Name Certificate**—If you want to do business under a fictitious name, you must file a certificate of that name with the county in which you will do business.

4. **Sales and Use Tax/Sales and Use Tax Exemption**—if you will be purchasing goods for resale, you should apply for a Sales and Use Tax Exemption Certificate before you start your business. You should not pay sales tax on goods when you purchase them for resale, because you will be required to collect and report Sales and Use Tax on the goods when you sell them. You can get the form for both the Sales and Use tax and the Sales and Use Tax Exemption Certificate at your state's website. You can find most state websites by entering **Sales and Use Tax (and your state's name)** in the Google search engine. State agencies collecting taxes go by different names. For example in Georgia, sales taxes are collected by the Georgia Department of Revenue. In California, Sales taxes are collected by The State Board of Equalization.

5. **Obtain Insurance**—You will need insurance on any vehicles used in your business as well as liability insurance for the premise if customers will be coming in. Consider hazard insurance and other types of insurance according to the risk factors of your business.

6. **IRS Publication**—Request Publication 334, Tax Guide for Small Business and Publication 583, Starting a Business and Keeping Records, and Publication 15, Employer's Tax Guide if you have employees. You can order the publications at irs.gov or call 1 (800) 829-3676.

Start-Up Checklist For Partnerships:

1. **Business License**—Obtain from the city or county in which you will do business.

2. **Employer Identification Number (EIN)**—Use IRS Form SS-4 to apply for an EIN. You can print the form at irs.gov, complete it, and call 1 (800) 829-4933 to get the EIN by phone or mail the application to the address on the form.

3. **Fictitious Name Certificate**—If you want to do business under a fictitious name, you must file a certificate of that name with the county in which you will do business. Some states require you to register with the secretary of state.

4. **Seller's Permit**—If you will be selling goods, you must apply for a state registration number as you will be required to collect and report the sales tax on the goods you sell. You do this by filing a State Tax Registration Application with the state in which you will do business.

5. **Business Bank Account**—Use your EIN and a copy of your partnership agreement to open the business bank account. You must decide who will sign the checks and how many signatures are required.

6. **Obtain Insurance**—You will need insurance on any vehicles used in your business as well as liability insurance for the premise if customers will be coming in. Consider hazard insurance and other types of insurance according to the risk factors of your business.

7. **Partnership Agreement**—As with any agreement among individuals, disputes will eventually arise. The best solution for this is a well written partnership agreement.

Start-Up Checklist For A Limited Liability Company:

The Start-up Checklist for a Limited Partnership is the same as for a General Partnership.

Start-Up Checklist For Corporations:

1. **Articles of Incorporation**—The incorporators will prepare and file the articles of incorporation with the secretary of state to set up the corporation.

2. **Business License**—Obtain from the city or county in which you will do business.

3. **Employer Identification Number (EIN)**—Use IRS Form SS-4 to apply for an EIN. You can print the form at irs.gov, complete it, and call 1 (800) 829-4933 to get the EIN by phone or mail the application to the address on the form.

4. **Fictitious Name Certificate**—If you want to do business under a fictitious name, you must register the name with the secretary of state. You should always use your official corporate name in conjunction with the fictitious name. i.e., The Velvet Butler, powered by The Velvet Touch, Inc.

5. **Elect the Board of Directors**—In some states, the board of directors are appointed by the incorporators and named in the articles of incorporation.

6. **Corporate Seal**—You can purchase a corporate kit which includes the corporate seal, bylaws, and stock certificates. Many small corporations choose not to order a corporate seal or kit. If you choose not to, you can use a loose leaf binder as your record book and prepare your own bylaws.

7. **Adopt Bylaws**—The bylaws serve as the corporation's internal manual. It sets forth the rules for holding meetings, electing officers and directors, and managing the business of the corporation. It also spells out the rights and powers of the corporation's shareholders, directors, and officers.

8. **Hold a Director's Meeting**—The board of directors will need to hold their first meeting, make a record of the meeting, and keep it in the corporate record book.

9. **Issue Stock**—The corporation should issue a stock certificate to each shareholder designating their ownership interest in the corporation. Blank stock certificates are usually included in the corporate record book. If you choose not to obtain a corporate kit, purchase your own stock certificates from an office supply store.

10. **Business Bank Account**—You will use your EIN to open your bank account. You must decide who will sign the checks and how many signatures will

WHAT YOU NEED TO KNOW BEFORE YOU START A BUSINESS

be required. You will also need a copy of the articles of incorporation.

11. **Obtain Insurance**—You will need an insurance program that covers all known risk factors for your corporation. Check first to see what the state law requires. You will want insurance on vehicles used in the business, workers compensation insurance if you have three or more employees, and general liability to cover all known risk factors for your business. Others types of insurances to consider are: tenant's insurance, product liability insurance, business interruption insurance, and theft insurance if employees handle or have access to money.

Start-Up Checklist For S Corporations:

The start-up checklist for an S corporation is pretty much the same as that for a regular corporation. The primary difference is that the S corporation must file IRS Form 2553 to make the election to become an S corporation.

Start-Up Checklist For Exempt Organizations:

1. **Articles of Incorporation**—The incorporators will prepare and file the articles of incorporation with the secretary of state to set up the corporation. A copy of the articles must be filed with your application for exempt status.

2. **Employer Identification Number**—Use IRS Form SS-4 to apply. You can get the form at irs.gov. You can complete the form and then call 1 (800) 829-4933 and give them the information from the form, and they will issue you a number by phone and give you instructions on how to mail the application.

3. File an application for exempt status under Internal Revenue Code Section 501(c)(3) using IRS Application 1023.

4. Pay a User Fee with the application of $300 if annual gross income is $10,000 during the 4 years before filing for exempt status. If you are just beginning, obviously, your gross income is less that $10,000. If your annual gross income is over $10,000, the User Fee is $750, and the amount for both will increase by $100 for applications filed after January 3, 2010.

5. **Elect the Board of Directors**—In some states, the board of directors are appointed by the incorporators and named in the articles of incorporation.

6. **Prepare and Adopt Bylaws**—The bylaws serve as the organization's internal manual. It governs the rules for holding meetings, electing officers and directors, and managing the business of the organization.

7. **Hold a Director's Meeting**—The board of directors will need to hold their first meeting, make a record of the meeting, and keep it in the corporate record book.

8. **Choose a Membership Structure**—If your organization is small, you may decide not to have members. It will be easier to set up and operate the organization without members.

9. **Corporate Seal**—A corporate seal is usually included in the corporate kit. Many small organizations choose not to order a corporate seal or kit. If you choose not to, you can use a loose leaf binder as your record book. Keep a record of all meetings in the record book.

10. **Business Bank Account**—You must decide who will sign the checks and how many signatures will be required. You will need a copy of your articles of incorporation to set up a new bank account.

11. **Obtain Insurance**—In order to insulate officers and directors from personal liability for actions taken on behalf of the organization, you will need to obtain Act and Omissions insurance. If this type insurance is out of your reach financially, officers and directors can protect themselves by insuring that the business is carried on as it should be and keeping abreast of all transactions of the organization. Of course, you will need insurance against obvious risks, such as coverage of vehicles and the organization's premise.

APPENDIX B
BUSINESS FORMS

Federal Form

Form SS-4 Application for Employer Identification Number

Georgia Forms
State Tax Exemption Form
State Tax Registrations

California Forms

BUSINESS FORMS

Federal Form

1. **SS-4: Application for Employer Identification Number (EIN)**

   There are several ways to get you EIN:

   - By Phone: Call IRS at 1(800) 829-3676 to request an SS-4 by mail or print the form from <u>www.irs. gov</u>. (To print the form from the IRS webpage, click on Forms and Publications in the box in the upper left corner. Then click on Forms and Publications in the body of the page. In the box that appears, type SS-4 and choose Product, then click search. When the link for the form appear, click it and print the form)

     - ▤ Once you have the form, complete the form and call IRS at (800) 829-1040 to have the number issued by phone

   - By Mail: Mail the completed SS-4 to the address on the form

   - By Fax: Complete the SS-4 and fax it to IRS at

   - Online: On the IRS webpage, click on Businesses in the upper left corner, then

     - ⌃ Click on More Topics in the box below businesses

     - ⌃ Scroll down and click on Employer ID Number (EIN)

  ⚲ Click on Apply Online and following the instructions

2. Form I-9: Employment Eligibility Verification

- All employees hired after November 6, 1986 mustc omplete form I-9 verifying that they are eligible to work in the United States. This form must be completed at the time you hire the individual.

- You can get a copy of this form at the U. S. Citizenship and Immigration Services website- www.uscis.gov/i-9. Once completed and signed by the employee, the employer must keep a copy for three years.

3. Form 8832: Election by a Small Business Corporation

- A one person LLC is automatically considers a sole proprietor by the IRS for income tax purposes. Likewise, a two-person LLC is considered a partnership.

- Form 8832 can be used by a one-person LLC to elect to file its tax return as a corporation rather than as a sole proprietor. It can also be used by a two-person LLC that wishes to file its tax return as a corporation rather than as a partnership.

START-UP FORMS YOU WILL NEED TO COMPLETE

Below is a list of forms you will need to start your business. These forms must be obtained from the issuing agency (City, County, or State). You may obtain many of the forms by going to the agency website.

You will be required to go into the office to complete certain forms. For example, most cities and counties require that you make a personal visit to the office to apply for a business license.

You will be able to obtain some forms from the agency website and complete and mail them in. You can locate the website by typing the form name and the name of the city, county or state in a search engine such as Google. I.e. State of Georgia Sales Tax Permit. From the website, you can usually print blank forms or complete the form online and print it. If you are unable to print the form, call the agency as ask to have the form mailed to you. The phone number is listed on the website.

- State Payroll Identification Number
- Business Fictitious Name Form
- State Sales Tax Permit
- City Business License or Permit
- County License or Permit

SPECIFIC GEORGIA FORMS

- **State Sales Tax Registration Form**

  You should apply for a State tax registration number before you begin selling products and services on which you will collect the sales tax. You are required to collect and pay a sales tax on retail sales. This is the number you will use to report the sales tax you collect on the goods you sell , as well as services you provide to your customers that involve the transfer of tangible personal property. You can get the application at www.dor.ga.gov.

  1. Click on forms and publications at the top of the page

  2. Scroll down and click on the first form CRF -002 Sales and Use Tax Registration Form.

- **Sales & Use Tax Certificate of Exemption**

  You should also apply for a Certificate of Exemption if you will be purchasing goods for resale. Otherwise you will have to pay the tax at the time of purchase and reimburse yourself by collecting the tax from the customer. You can get the form at www.dor.ga.gov.

  1. Click on forms and publications at the top of the page

  2. Click on ST-5 Sales and Use Tax Certificate of Exemption

- If you have a non-profit or charitable organization, you may use your letter of Determination from the IRS to show that you are exempt from paying sales tax on goods you purchase for the organization's use.

- **Form ST-3 Sales & Use Tax**

Use his form to report taxes you collect on good and services you sell in Georgia. You can print the form at www.dor.gov or call (877) 423-6711.

If you have questions about the forms, you can get help by calling (877)-423-6711.

SPECIFIC CALIFORNIA FORMS

Federal Form

- **SS-4:** Application for Employer Identification Number (EIN) This form is the same for all states. For full details and explanation, (See federal Form listed in Appendix B under Business Form

- **Los Angeles County Business License and Permit**: Visit www.calgold.ca.gov

- **Fictitious Business Name (FBN):** Visit www.regrec.co.la.ca.us. Telephone number: 562-462-2056

  Zoning Information: 213-974-6443. Request by fax, 213-626-0434. Email: zoningldcc@planning.co.la.ca.us

  California State Board Of Equalization (Sellers Permit). Telephone number: 800-400-7115. Website: www.boe.ca.gov

Breinigsville, PA USA
22 April 2010
236638BV00001B/18/P